SPIRIT AND I

Christine Stewart

Published by New Generation Publishing in 2021

Copyright © Christine Stewart 2021

First Edition

ISBN   978-1-80369-066-7

Cover artwork by Nick Peill

www.newgeneration-publishing.com

New Generation Publishing

SPIRIT AND I

My life and how my Spirituality developed.

Thanks to my lovely family who support me in all I do, even though they call me a witch.

I needed to express my feelings and get on with my life, but I find often I am looking backwards, I should not though I should be going forward learning as I develop my Mediumship. I take life as it is and the challenges that have happened during my life makes me the better person.

My family are my strength especially my husband Peter as in the bible he is my rock. We have been together 31 years we have had our ups and downs, illness and upset but we have weathered the storm.

I spend many hours looking into what to do next, but at the end of the day I find myself. And now know what life holds for me it will be guided by Spirit. I am appreciative and love my life now.

We have lost 3 members of our family which is distressing to say the least. Alan was the first, followed by Angelo and then Colin in 2020. None of them reached old age.

I saw that other mediums had written their own books, and also, I could claim I was an international medium so thought Why Not.

Opening to Life

1

*Life holds many invaluable mysteries which we tend to
share and grow.*

I began my life in the beautiful city of York on 13th
October 1945 to a single woman Olive Elsie Barker, my
father was a Canadian Air force pilot stationed at Fulford
York who I never knew so what I didn't know I did not
miss. My grandfather wanted my mother to give me up
and put me in a Dr Barnados Home my mother refused.
Sometimes I wonder how things would have turned out if
she had.

Before long she was pregnant again, my grandparents
looked after me and my mother was sent to an unmarried
mother's home at Hornsea on the Yorkshire coast where
she gave birth to my sister Jacqueline, September 6th,
1947.

My earliest memories were going to a flat and being
looked after by a young woman and man who I later found
was my Uncle David, mums brother and his then girlfriend
Mavis, I was eighteen months old. Then traveling on a bus
with my grandmother to my aunty Dories I was three. She
was an intimidating person I had to be seen and not heard.
I used to hide behind the chair.

We then moved to a village in Lincolnshire Misterton my
mum had friends there, she started working at Roses in
Gainsborough. First, I fell into the fire from my highchair
good job I was grabbed, and then run over by a milk float
again luck. We then moved to Gainsborough to North

Marsh Road Gainsborough to someone I called aunty Lily, it was then my mum met and married my stepfather,

My next memory was being four and going to a nursery school, also being always in trouble with the man my mother married, my life changed and sometimes I wonder if I would have been better off being farmed out but then I would not have had the experiences that life has given me. I know I always seemed to be afraid and had a stammer which when I was agitated would be more pronounced.

The next was going to school and instead of going home, I played with my friends. It was dark so instead of going home I sat on the doorstep next door. My mother put the milk bottles out I spoke to her, she took me inside my stepfather gave me the hiding of my life, I guess I deserved it I never stayed out again,

My Next memory was to be taken to a hospital to have an abscess lanced in my throat under general anesthetic which I later learned was Scunthorpe General Hospital, where I was taken to the waiting room and some kindly lady had given me some chocolate before my anesthetic and suffice to say I was violently sick.

We lived in rooms in Gainsborough Britannia Cottages, again it was a time where my stepfather was quite tough with me, I was shipped of to York to my grandmothers while my mother had the third baby. Unfortunately, my sister Patricia was born December 29th 1949 6 hours later she passed away.

I was brought home from York and started infant school. I was 4 and a half. We then moved into Nissen huts on lea road, again shipped off to York while my mum had my brother Keith, Then brother Brian. I loved being in York my grandma and grandad doted on me. I had my own room which was decorated for a little girl.

I was born with a heart defect and from an early age was always told I had to take things easy, I also spent a lot of time backwards and forwards to the hospital for checkups. Also, I had lots of Migraine headaches which caused lots of missing school, but I am sure lots of these could have been prevented by anxiety and food issues, such as chocolate and cheese.

But then again as we know now life has many things in store for us and we learn from the many books of life, each of us has our own pathway to walk along with obstacles and twists and turns, with most of us being able to pack lots and lots of wonderful events into our lives and see many changes.

Then it was a time of change we were re-housed it the uphill in Gainsborough Highfield close, my mother loved it we had a lovely, polished home, but dad decided he didn't like it so he moved us to 64 Trinity Street a rambling house, haunted with black clock beetles and rats out the back, a right hovel but it was home. Then things changed I became withdrawn; my stepfather took an unnatural interest in me. I used to hide away. But because he said I would have to be sent into a Dr Banados home I kept quiet.

I had an extremely hard life which I do not want to elaborate on but just to say my life held many happenings which I regret and wish to forget. Because it could harm many people and what has passed has gone. I learned from an early age to hide my feelings and the hurt inside, and when I suffered disillusionment, I would close myself within a fantasy world with what if? and I would close myself in my own dream world.

I saw lots of spirit people when I closed my eyes, they were my comfort I did not know they were spirit. I think that is why I am a good spiritual teacher I have dealt with my own issues and learnt to live with them.

My Mother was a lovely gentle lady but was too soft maybe if she had not married, she would still be alive, but it is no good saying what if! She fell ill when I was fourteen and then I had to swiftly grow up, my life changed, I had to raise my younger brothers and sisters with the help of Jackie, but she suffered the same as me. I left school at fifteen got my first job which I had to leave to take over our shop and help my mother. My sister had more strength than me she learned to say no and left home at seventeen she escaped.

Our life had changed dramatically, after she left, I had the shop to look after, cook, clean, and ensure the lads and Sandra were clean to go to school, as well as working full time as well. Sandra had to help but as she was his daughter she got away with a lot.

One time I had to fetch Sandra home from school as she had fallen, I did not bring her straight home, and it was found her arm was broken. I got thumped, all in the day of the life of a skivvy.

Mum did manage to go to bingo at the Kings Theatre, with her friend Joan Broadberry, when she won all was well in the house because she shared her winnings with him.

And so, I grew

2

To learn is to grow and to be whole

I met a man, called John but had so much going on trouble at home, with him, and desperation with not being able to be a child have freedom, wanting so much to have a life of my own, I took to not washing I thought that if I was dirty nobody would look at me, which was stupid when I think back. I was allowed to go to the pictures with my friends once a week, Janet and Maisie I used to enjoy those nights.

I tried to take my own life, but fortunately my mother found me, I was taken to the hospital, had my stomach pumped It was so degrading I must have been desperate, but I know it was a cry for help, but I never did get any because I never told a soul of what I was going through.

It took many years before I was given the help I needed. And that took courage and lots of understanding from my family which was extremely hard, to talk about, and sometimes when I look back, I can see my mistakes and see when the healing began.

I started work at a underwear factory making lace for brassieres not very nice, but had to return to look after the shop and cook and clean. Dad then came back from lorry driving to start a printing business from home.

I then got a job at Wolsey and loved it, I made lots of friends, I stayed there for three years, when I married 11th April 1964 for the first time to a man my own age William Charles Gagg (Bill) I must add to get away from home,

The nurse at Wolsey gave me a pink cocktail dress for my wedding and another friend made me a veil with a tiara, all my family from York came but not my sister Jackie she was made to look after the shop. I walked home from the reception in my wedding finery so she could see me and Sandra as my bridesmaid.

After my wedding we lived with my family until we got our own place, but worries and arguments, we left and went to Bills Mothers which was a relief. I worried about my mum as her health was not good, but I had to get away.

We moved to Broughton near Brigg, Bill got a job which he didn't like, I got a job in a knitwear factory which was ok, but Bill wanted to move out of his mothers. So packed our belongings and moved to a tied cottage in Christchurch in Cambridgeshire, where his mother and father came and moved into another tied cottage, We seemed to settle down but again he got itchy feet, so belongings packed we where on the move again.

This time we moved to Chettisham near Ely, but my marriage was not to last, we had moved backwards and forwards living in tied cottages, no money and not being happy.

I had a miscarriage September 1964 as I did not know I was pregnant I was working on the land and not looking after me. My neighbor in Chettisham near Ely helped me clean up and made sure I was alright.

My mother was taken seriously ill in December 1964 I went home and never went back. Knowing what was to come would I have left, or would I have stuck it out? we learn from our mistakes.

Many things happened from then I went wild and found myself pregnant to a chap who did not really want me.

And I did not really like him. but after a simple birth June my daughter was born 15th March 1966, she was so beautiful with the most enormous brown eyes, I loved her from the moment I saw her.

I still had many issues with myself and when June was three months old my husband Bill came back into my life, he accepted June as his own and we tried to make a go of our marriage, which was at first like a second honeymoon but the cracks where showing. He was a womanizer and hated responsibility which was a shame he was a nice man, but family was not his forte.

We moved into a small, terraced house in Cross Street Gainsborough, We paid 7s/6p a week for this house but it was cold and damp. We then packed up and then moved into a small house in Malpas avenue where on 18th March 1968 I gave birth to my son Christopher, he never stopped crying for about two and a half months this strained our marriage to breaking point, but we survived.

Bill was having an affair with my friend, which I found out later which again made a strained marriage, I never let him know I knew.

Bill had a couple of jobs and did not like either, so we decided to take the kids and move to Three Holes in Cambridgeshire he had hitchhiked down and got a job on a farm the cottage was a tied cottage which went with the job, we stayed there about six months. Bill got itchy feet again he resigned his job, so we had to give up the house, this time we moved for three weeks into his mother's house, his father did not want us there. And made his feeling known.

My mother died 8th December 1968 we went back for the funeral left June and Christopher with his mother. When we got back Bills dad told us to find somewhere else to live.

Bill got a job on the land again laying cables this time we moved onto a caravan site in Wisbech, I was about six months pregnant.

I gave birth to my daughter Amanda on 10th September 1969 she was a quiet baby no trouble ate and slept which was nice. But unfortunately, my husband was playing around again with one of my neighbors' so that was the end of my marriage.

I was at the end of my tether did I go home to Gainsborough or did I look for somewhere to rent. I saw an advert for breakfast cook with accommodation just down the road.

I moved with the three children to the Glendon Hotel which had a caravan site I was given the caravan for working in the hotel as a breakfast cook, which suited me as the girl who lived in the next caravan kept an ear to my children.

The Hotel was particularly good to me they gave me meals for the children and bits and pieces we survived well and because my neighbour was a good friend, we shared the food, and we saved a little money which was great. It was not to last though.

I spent a lot of time in the hotel the owner let me have baths and showers which was brilliant. Although we lived in the caravan it was good to be able to keep us clean. My stepfather came and asked me to move back to Gainsborough he said it would be better for the kids. I declined It would give him free rein to go back to his old ways.

I loved to go out first thing in the morning to walk into town and meet up with friends I had made. I would stay with the kids until it was dark.

There was a little café where you could sit, and nobody threw you out.

I made a few friends which was nice, but I felt a little niggle at the back of mind that all was not well. I was not feeling well and being sick. I had Hemorrhaged after the birth of Amanda so went to the doctors.

My blood iron was low, and I had an infection which was making me ill. I was given a course of Iron tablets and antibiotics which thank goodness worked. But I was smoking too much and with always having a bad chest I was stupid. So that November I had a bad case of bronchitis.

I also had been having nightmares and worrying about how my life's path had gone, looking back, and seeing what if again? But I knew I had to overcome my difficulties, I just had to believe in myself again, I had post-natal depression.

I was thinking again about the past and how things had been and then when I found my sister had been put into care. I found myself and decided nobody would hurt me again. There was no way to contact her so I worried about her too.

I found out also Bill was lorry driving and was staying at Gainsborough and blaming me for the breakup of our marriage. As I said you can only take so much infidelity so I let it go and told my brothers I was a stronger more adaptable person and to tell him I was going for full custody and a divorce. I never heard from him again.

New Start

3

New doors opening finding choices

January 1970 was a strange time I met my future husband Alan he was a Jack the lad and I didn't really like him a lot, but he made me laugh. We played cards and monopoly with his brother and then girlfriend Pam who lived in the caravans around the corner,

I met them as I got my pram stuck in mud and snow, He took to my kids and although he was divorced, he was trying to get his children from his ex-wife. If I knew then what I know now it would not have continued. Our lives are mapped, I believe.

We decided to get together at Easter and moved up to Liverpool so we could see his kids and maybe sort something out, for access of his sons then eight five and three. Another move into a maisonet in Kirby on a bad estate with lots of trouble. We had Peter and John then Little Alan.

My stepfather asked us to come back from Liverpool and take over the shop. Which we did. Alan worked at Marshalls the big machinery factory as a Fettler, I looked after the shop and added new stock so that the shop was viable. The takings has gone up.

We were there three months when my stepfather started to act weirdly, Alan had painted the place out ready for us to take over and we pay him rent. Also, to give a home to my two brothers Brian and Raymond.

A big row the kids upset, and Christopher fell downstairs all hectic, so we decided to leave. We caught a train to March then to Wisbech again we had come full circle.

My stepfather now the shop was painted out, and ready for new owners he sold the shop and house and left my brothers homeless. Married the woman he had met and moves to Handsworth. A chapter ended.

We had stayed in Liverpool for a year and by the time we went back down south we had Alan's three boys as well as my own three. At Gainsborough there was enough room for us all, so the boys started school and seemed to be ok.

But then as I said before with my stepfather being secretive and causing arguments it was time to go. He was also seeing a woman from Birmingham, so he wanted out. Then I found I was pregnant, of which I did not carry her very well I was always ill and bleeding off and on. Coming away from Gainsborough was the best thing as I knew I would not have carried her as it was a stressful time.

We were at the Glendon Hotel again with me pregnant and working as a five thirty breakfast cook for the fishermen, when I went into premature Labour and gave birth to Suzanne 9th June 1971 two months early. She was a sickly baby it took all my time to feed her, but she survived.

Alan I Suzanne and Young Alan (as he was a bad asthmatic) lived in the caravan, whilst the kids slept in a shed, it was warm and cozy but was not suitable. Christopher started sleep walking and as there was a pond it was not really a great thing to be away from me. So had to lock the shed. Spoke to the health visitor, she contacted social services.

I met a lovely lady she took a liking to me and would often cook me a dinner, so I could have time away from the kids. Her name was Zillah. Plumb. She was a real spiritual lady who read the bible daily. She bought me a lovely bible, and she gave me passages to read to help with my depression. She saved my life.

She was not happy with me living in sin she said it demined my soul, She gave me the money for our marriage license. So as I was waiting for my decree Absolute I kept the money safe.

One month later we moved into a council house on Garden Lane Wisbech St Mary it was lovely I loved it, but Alan hated it and after we married 19th November 1971, he always found reasons why we couldn't stay there and after causing problems with the neighbours we moved from Wisbech St Mary to Ely and stayed in and around Ely until Alan died in 1986.

We stayed with his brother and wife all was up and down but arguments and other issues. I had a job at the plastics factory in the morning, and Alan did the night shift. Pam looked after the kids, and then I looked after hers as well on the evenings. Until the blow up with Paul my brother-in-law.

We were made homeless and had to go into a hostel in Linton near Cambridge. I got a job in the fish and chip shop in Linton as a temp until we got a house. We were given a temporary home in Downham Road Ely. The kids were able to go to school at St Mary's at Ely.

This was were the first issues of illness were shown and worries with young Alan with asthma. He was sent to the sea-side Eden Hall it was like a sanitorium a place for healing, but he ran away, and hitch-hiked home. The council put us on the top of the list so we were awaiting a place to move too.

This was a trying time we moved from Downham Road Ely to Prickwillow, and then to High Barns Ely each move was supposed to better us, it was a time of growing for all the kids, they fought like all kids did but they grew up in to fine adults and I was incredibly pleased with the outcome.

Alan never stood still, and he was a person who changed beyond recognition, he was secretive and was not a genuinely nice man whom we found out about later, my daughters June and Amanda whom I found out about later, suffered so much at his hands

I wish to God I had got out but as the Spirit says what goes around comes around. I am a big believer in this; also, God does not pay his debts with money. I would have left him and made a new life, but this is not about him it is about my life.

My sister Sandra came to visit with her friend I hadn't seen her for a while as issues with her and my stepfather where ongoing she was on her way to Waterbeach where she was meeting her fiancé a soldier in the army from Plymouth thank goodness she had got away. Next, I heard she had married with none of her family with her.

Alan and I did a lot of work on the land strawberry picking, and onion picking, he would then use the money for his bets, he was a gambler, and liked a pint or two. He did win sometime which was good as he always brought back a gift for the kids and flowers for me.

The children grew and as a family we survived, we had my brother Keith living with us, both Alan and Keith worked at the sugar beet factory in Queen Adelaide, it was only for the winter months, but we were able to save a little money which helped a great deal, filled the freezers for Christmas. The cold was always bitter living out in the wilds which did not help with Alan's health he was often chesty so probably this was the starting of his lung cancer.

At this time, I was working at different jobs to help make ends meet, next door was a garage which belonged to a farm, I worked there when there was a job potato picking setting and riddling. Strawberry apple and plum picking. Also. I was always tired and often walked the 4 miles to Ely to get essential shopping and get the bus back, sometimes he would come too to have is bet.

I worked at the Northampton Boot Factory as a machinist, when there was no land work, also as a cook at the Still and Sugar Loaf. Keith had a girlfriend Evelyn Main she stayed at our house with him, so I had my lift back and forward to work I loved the job.

We also Joined the ladies dart team at the White Hart in Ely, and I won a few trophies. Alan also played for the men's team and for The Prince Albert with his brother Paul. We had lots of friends who helped us to enjoy ourselves and keep us sane.

Just before the winter intake for the sugar beet factory, Alans's brother David came down a stayed with us, He got a job at the cardboard factory and lived with us until Easter, He then got a flat in Ely and started working at Jardins at Sutton. Our house was open house.

The council decided they were going to sell our house and offered us a house in Ely which we took as little Alan was leaving school and the other kids as they grew would be nearer to the town to get jobs. The house was four bedrooms on an estate and was not too bad. This time June was living in Margate things out of my control, but at least she was safe.

During the time he was not working at the beet factory: Alan started working part time for a removal firm Casson's Dave and Rita were to become good friends of our and always made sure there was a job. Dave sent me on a job at the jam factory which was an experience, and I received a wage.

We all worked hard keeping the family together. Alan was very ill all the winter, but he went to work with Keith, but the cough was getting worse, yet he was still smoking.

In February he had to collect his wages from the sugar beet factory. We caught the bus to Queen Adelaide at 12 o'clock when the weather changed to a blizzard all the busses had stopped so we had to walk home, it was three miles he was so ill and ended up with bronchitis. He was sent for an Xray which was inconclusive, This was February 1985, then in July 1985 he was sent to Papworth Hospital a large growth was found in Alan's lung all the strength was needed then.

My brother Raymond (Ben) came to visit and got a job at Jardins with David. He also got a flat on the high street in Sutton rented of the Nun family. He had an accident on a motorbike broke his leg and was in hospital for 13 weeks. When he came out his flat had gone so he decided to go back to Gainsborough.

Alans brother Paul lived across the road from us with his wife and kids, what a funny man he was always an angry man. He took a lot in his head that we had done him wrong so would cut us dead. It would be funny but was so pathetic. He would tell his wife Pam if she spoke to us she would be out on her ear.

Strange, strange man. Yet when push came to shove, he was a godsend when Alan was dying.

Again, it was a time of change learning for me and a strength I did not know I had, made me stronger. As all I had gone through in life was there had to be a happier time?

It took its toll will me I seemed to be always tired, maybe because I was always on the go. But the friends I had always knew when I needed help.

Alan and Belinda got married with Alan being ok to attend the wedding, but he looked gaunt. I knew there was something seriously wrong, so this was when he was taken into Papworth hospital for tests. The cancer had spread.

We were backwards and forwards to the hospital and in September, Alan went to bed and found he was paralyzed from the waist down. I just sat a cried and cried. Nobody ever saw me I just went upstairs locked the bathroom door and cried. A friend Val Woodbine helped me to cry and hide my emotions.

Val found me in the phone box near the cemetery sobbing my heart out, I had just phoned the doctor for results he said 3 months that was all they gave him. I asked the doctor not to tell him let him hope. Was I right or was I wrong?

We had a wonderful Doctor his name was Doctor Woods. He helped me and got things done. Our previous Doctor had died so we moved to a different practice which was a Gods send. The nurses and health visitors helped so much.

From September until December the time went in a blur nothing seemed to be working. Alan took it on himself to get the Christmas presents from John Moores Catalogue.

Usually, they had so many presents it was silly this year they had one big present and just a few little ones. I took him out in his wheelchair, we bought the small gifts from Woolworths. And he wrapped them for something to do .

Belinda and Alan meanwhile had a daughter Lucy Tara beautiful little girl. Alan was able to spend time with her. Alan and Belinda would bring Lucy from Cambridge to see him once a week. Also David and Paul would come in daily to give him upliftment.

Spiritual Door Knocking

4

Spirit holds court and teaches us lessons which help us to
spiritual growth

My first encounter with the spirit world was when I was seven although I did not realize this until I was older, we lived at a house in Gainsborough 64 Trinity Street both my sister and I shared the attic room which was quite gloomy, we used to run up the stairs like bats out of hell as we always saw a shadowy figure at the second landing, and we always felt ourselves pushed. Yet it was not a bad place.

We would hear rapping and tapping in the middle of the night, we would tap back and so the game continued. We thought it was the boys next door. Then one night we tapped back, and it could not have been the boys they were on holiday, we never tapped anymore after that.

My second was at Christchurch in Cambridgeshire in 1964 we lived at Poppy Tree Farm and spent part of the day at Bills Mothers house and when we went home, we would hear footsteps walking in the bedroom and nobody there when we checked, Music being played just out of ear shot.

One day the door opened the footsteps came and stopped outside the door a knock and nobody there when the door was opened, but it wasn't unpleasant. Also, in his mother's house I felt someone come past me in the stairwell pushing and shoving just letting us know they were around.

My third encounter with Spirit was 1968 at Poplar Farm Emneth Wisbech when my first husband and I stayed with his family, I had not long given birth to Christopher he would have been around three and a half months old,

I was sleeping between feeds and it was about two thirty in the morning I woke to a strange half light and was watching an old man of about 70 to 75 carving an animal out of a small piece of wood he was smoking a pipe, I watched him for a while marveling at his skill. He then started to mend shoes and he kept tap, tap, tapping which I thought someone is going to hear this, but they did not. Then as he turned towards me, he grinned and disappeared, I never forgot that.

I had my next encounter with the spirit world in 1973 when I lived on Downham Road we went around to a woman at the end house Kath Haigh she had a séance and invited me in. , this was a time of learning for me as I did not know what was happening, she had darkened the room, placed candles, placed letters of the alphabet, and placed a glass on the table with a yes and a no. There were six of us sat around this table plus Kath she had just lost her son and wanted to contact him.

It was strange really because I did not know what was going to happen, so I was skeptical as it was. We all placed a finger on the glass and asked if anyone was there the glass moved but I smiled to myself I was sure someone was pushing it. Then suddenly, the glass flew of the table and smashed on the wall, I was gone out of the door like a shot with all the others behind me, I have never done anything like that again.

Also, at, this time, we were seeing shapes in the rooms, in Downham Road someone or something just out eyeshot. Sometimes a figure standing in the doorway the children waking up scared an apparition over in the corner of the room just forming and a feeling of nausea. As I realized later it was me opening to spirit, again I did not understand.

We asked to be moved, the Council gave us The Old Police House Prickwillow, now this was a house where we not only saw spirit each one of the kids saw or had some experience, but nothing bad we were happy there. And this was where we stayed for four years, I met quite a few good friends who I am still in contact with to this day even though we are miles apart.

Over the years I had many experiences which some stayed with me but when I think back, I had disregarded them as fantasy but now know better. I had a few odd things happen but did not think about them too deeply as it was not unpleasant, just saw shadowy people in passing and footsteps tramping up and down stairs. Also, things happening which I knew had happened before, and odd dreams which came true.

One was when we lived in Prickwillow a beautiful old Police house activity always began around November time, we would go to bed lock the front door, but every morning the door would be open, we would see a shadowy person standing at the top of the stairs. A cold, blast would whistle round the house and cause a chill, no matter how high the fire was. The boys would come flying down the stairs saying there was an old woman looking at them. We would say no they were imagining it.

But always on December 1st activity would cease. On talking to the people who knew the house would say a lady died in November. Also, someone had died tragically there as well so lots of spirits around. Again, it was not unpleasant but was unnerving to say the least.

I had one experience much later which knocked me for six. I was in Canada in 2005. My friend Rita arranged a circle for me to sit in with friends. Rita had been sitting for physical, so I was up for it. We all settled down and suddenly, a scream a banging and something went straight through me. The feeling was amazing the woman had been murdered by being thrown downstairs. Then a feeling of flies or something walking on my right arm I opened my eyes nothing there but finger marks on my arm. I would love to experience again.

Things whereas I could only say different as I grew older and the way my life was also changing my family life was disrupted, when Alan was diagnosed with lung cancer in July 1985 at Papworth Hospital Cambridge, we were positive, the doctors said they would try a new drug on him called inferron this accelerated the cancer, September 1985 as I said before, the cancer affected his lower spine, and he was paralyzed from the waist downwards. These were secondaries.

This was a time of learning, learning how to cope. This was extremely hard, backwards and forwards to hospital losing direction but not giving up. Kids' out of hand not wanting to be in a house of illness, tears and tantrums, my God that was a hard time. This was a very trying time June had come home at Christmas I don't know what she said to him, but I knew she was going to come home when he died, I decided not to let him go into a hospice Dr Woods in Ely was so good to us and the Macmillan nurses where positive angels helping and supporting, a time of learning. Alan took a turn for the worse on Boxing Day but rallied round and started to put a bit of weight on. I was his carer and nurse which sometimes was hard, very, very hard. I never minded though.

His mother Kitty {Catherine Doran} came to stay with us the middle of January to give him a little positivity and he really did start to look better. By support and helping him to pick a bet a day kept his mind busy.

On 24th January 1986 Alan woke at 4 am and started to laugh he said there was a white cat on my shoulder and twin girls waiting for him. This freaked me out as I knew his mother had lost twins, but I thought he was hallucinating, so next morning I went to the Catholic Church and asked the priest to visit him as he was Catholic. The priest came heard his confession and gave him the last rights.

His brothers and Sisters came to see him and as they arrived, Alan rallied again and on Saturday his family left. He seemed quite happy and spent time talking to his sons and allowed the girls to come and sit by him and read to him, it was peaceful.

On Tuesday 28th January he woke at 4 am again told me the twins were there and that he would be going with them at 8 o'clock I contacted the family again and they all returned because they had gone back to Liverpool.

The priest came again that morning too and prayed with him he seemed more relaxed.

His mum sat with Alan all day holding his hand talking to him. his niece Lois came he became anxious he shouted at her and told her to move her car as his car could not come for him. Lois had to go outside and move her car, he then calmed down.

His brothers David and Paul popped in and out to the bookies, and at 6 o'clock they sat with him too, Alan died at 8pm Tuesday 28th January 1986.With his mother his brothers and me present and I saw him go.

His youngest son my stepson John was a godsend that night he helped with the younger girls he took them to a neighbor until the funeral directors came. He just literally

22

took charge and ensured I was alright; the elder boys were out playing darts John rang to pubs where they were playing to tell them.

The family all rallied round and helped organize the funeral especially Paul and David Alan's brothers; His funeral was at the catholic church on 4th February. I lost three stone in weight in ten days, I think it was sadness and rushing around. But I always sensed Alan had not gone. Anywhere.

My daughter Amanda saw him a couple of times in the house, so she was Psychic as well but never acknowledges it. This was to be a time of change, but we never acknowledged it. She said he told her not to wake me as she was going to tell me he was back.

My next encounter was 7am 29th January 1986 Alan died 28th January at 8pm I felt the touch of a hand on my face saw a light then his photo fell of the mantelpiece. I felt him all around me, which was a different feeling altogether. This did not freak me out as this time, and I suppose I got and experienced comfort. Then at his funeral again lights and a feeling all was well.

Life Continues

5

Life continues at breakneck speed, but we endure

I spent time out with my girls going to the beet club and playing darts for the Highflyer with the ladies. Also, Dominoes and crib with my partner Eric Phillips. We would often go to Erics and Mary's after the beet club for supper. The girls loved going.

I went out with a man that time Gordon Taylor, I met him on rebound so did not last. Yet his family were very good with the girls and ensured they had a good Christmas. I was working at The Tower Hospital. Suzanne and Amanda decided to go to a party I was besides myself with worry.

All in a day in the life of me. I had a job in the Tower Hospital as a kitchen porter for 10 hours a week but managed to get promoted to assistant chef with Donny Rose and Bill It was a lovely job.

Nothing else did (or if it did I do not remember) happen for seven years I had a period of many changes around me hurt and I suppose déjà vu it (has happened before) I met and lived with a chap who was playing away from home so the need to break free came strongly I made the move back to Lincoln Lincolnshire where I met and married my present husband Peter who has been my strength and support for the last 31 years.

I couldn't move my shoulder at work in 1990 I was diagnosed with frozen shoulders or so we though but was a displacement of the bone and shoulder from a car accident in 1974 which was causing the wear and tear of the shoulders

In the ensuing two years I had three operations to rectify the damage, on which I was told I would be disabled as my arms would not work properly, the pain I suffered was unimaginable and was told I would never work again. So, what was I to do?

I spent hundreds of pounds going backwards and forwards to Sheffield to see a Chiropractitioner, after ten sessions they said they couldn't fix me so I was disabled.

My Stepdaughters Maria, Louise and friends often came one day in a week and helped to clean my house as I could not do it, I became awfully close with Maria and often I would go to her house for lunch, and to talk over what was going on in my life.

Whilst we were talking, I experienced my next spirit encounter I was talking to her when suddenly, her shape and face changed into that of my mother, at first, I was so shocked as I just sat mesmerized with what I was seeing, I then bolted out of the house to the car as Pete had just arrived to take me home. I said to him your daughter is weird lets go. Maria came outside laughing and said "did you have a Strange experience" we just left

My God the horror I felt how this could be… an ordinary lunch date talking to a person who I loved and respected and seeing a paranormal occurrence at twelve thirty lunch time.

When I think back now, it was so amazing and would happen again, and again and over the ensuing years has done, not only in company but in churches and in demonstrations. And to this day I often see Spirit people standing next to the person I am talking to.

One of the most significant was a man standing at the back of the church in Scunthorpe by the door and standing smiling at me whilst I was talking to his wife, I was able to describe him and give positive evidence as he had died in the war. The most significant was stealing a chicken on a nest of eggs for his wife. He brought the whole lot home where she reared the chicks and ate the chicken.

My stepdaughter Maria was a Godsend she helped me so much keeping body and soul clean and together helping me to go forward, her idea was to take me to the local Spiritualist Church for Healing she said what have you got to lose? So we went, the healer was a man named John Hardy he was a teacher trainer under the Tuition of Maurice Hutchinson, an extraordinarily strong healer who was to be my mentor and teacher with his wife Sally who was a good friend.

John asked me to sit on a stool and accept the healing as it was given, I touched John's hand and we experienced a bolt of electricity between us and heat which went up my arms into my shoulders, John said when you are healed, we need you to use the gift you have will you join us and train as a healer. I said yes.

For the next year I spent my Wednesday nights healing and being healed and was so grateful to be able to move my arms again so went back to work as a Taxi controller for Sam's Taxi's where I stayed for nine months but I needed more my brain was alive and needed stimulation.

I did not know this was Spirit taking me forward. So went to college to train for NVQ's in Administration which I passed level 1 and level 2. And my first proper job was with Translinc a subsidiary of Lincoln County Council where I stayed for two and a half years until the Management buyout, I was made redundant on 17th September 1997.

26

They gave me time off to look for another job, the first interview I had, I felt a connection with the interviewer, we had so much to talk about spiritually. Subsequently I began to work for Mastercare Service and Distribution (Dixons) on 19th September 1997 until I retired in November 2010.

This time was a time of great Transition moving from what I knew into the unknown as I began my development in earnest. I had begun my healer training in 1994 and sat in the Wednesday circle at the church for development no joy I saw and felt nothing for at least the first year. I was working at Translinc at the time and every morning would walk the mile to work learning as I walked the healing hymn, so I knew it off by heart.

Healing Hymn

Gracious Spirit of thy goodness
Hear our anxious prayer,
Take our love ones who are suffering
Neath thy tender care
Gracious spirit hear us hear us.

Gracious spirit may thy presence
Shed a healing ray
Turning all our nights of darkness,
Into glorious day
Gracious spirits hear us, hear us.

Gracious spirit should thou claim them
Be their light and guide
Lead them to thy heavenly kingdom
Safely by thy side.
Gracious spirit hear us hear us
Amen

Making the changes

6

Opening to the spirit and finding my way

At this time, I met Pat Brown who was known to me from the Church, she was taking spiritual development near Skegness with Pat and Elsie Ellis, she passed all her notes onto me which I typed up and devoured each lesson avidly, Pete bought me my first computer as I was typing it all up on a typewriter. He had it made from a man who made computers.

I learned, and I developed. I also sat in a circle with a close friend Lynne Merrills, she was a strong trance medium, also for a time with Maria until she left to go to university, and Paul Rasen we learned no end from Lynne she was our development. We did this for five years until I had my heart attack in 1999. Then the following year I began to work as a platform medium, a new beginning.

I saw my first spirit whilst healing in 1996 I was sitting holding the patients hands, just aware when I saw a bed with a patient laying flat it was quite grey but as I looked the doctor who was attending the patient looked at me and showed me the stomach area I could see a lump, the doctor placed his hands on the patient it then faded and I was left just holding the patients hands a young woman. I placed my hands on the patient's stomach and felt a trembling in this area then peace. The patient is still alive and well having had stomach surgery. So, I was shown what to do and how to do it.

After this I saw lots of things and always had a sense of knowing what was happening and when. My next encounter was 18th October 1997 my sister-in-law Jean was in Lincoln hospital after suffering a stroke I was aware of a clock ticking and it being 7 pm I knew I had to be at the hospital as she was going to pass over at 7 pm and she did I was with her as she took her transition.

That night I was shown a wide-open eye and told I had choices to make to either go with the eye or close it permanently, I chose open and from then on, I have worked with the spirit world they have let me experience many things and I still am experiencing these.

After this I was awoken time and time and again, with pictures, symbols, and words like a silent film. I asked them to slow it down so as I could take it all in. One night I was shown a road a bridge and a car, I saw the car crash into another and go off the road. I was so tired I asked what it was all about but got no answer. The next morning on the news a car had smashed near Cherry Willingham and gone over the bridge. Premonition?

I went with Lynne to Louth Church for a workshop with Gordon Smith the Scottish medium, and another medium. We sat in the circle he passed us all a sealed envelope, He asked us to feel the envelope and tell him what impressions we got from it. When it was my turn, I told him all I saw was sand and a pyramid. He said correct it was sand from the Sahara Desert.

Again, we went to another workshop in our own church with a medium from London. He blindfolded me and Ann Eameson, I was giving messages to the circle accurate and to the point. Ann took on the persona of the spirit person this was 1997 I had said I was getting nothing, but I certainly was.

A few weeks later we went back to Louth Shirley invited us to sit with Jean Skinner as we had bought tickets to see her Transfiguration demonstration. Jean took us on a walk through an Indian reservation to be introduced to our guides. Only it could happen to me a one-eyed, one-legged guide called Broken Arrow.

This was a funny year I had been working as a label and clerical assistant at Mastercare for a year and had been promoted to an Administrator in November which I enjoyed very much. I took over the fishing club, and then joined the entertainment committee.

My sister-in-law Evelyn asked me to give her a reading I hadn't done one before, so I said no. But she gave me an envelope I closed my eyes and saw a number 7 a path going down to water which was lake Gilped. I saw a man who I found out later was her dad. His birthday was 7th October and he lived by lake Gilped.

The same time we went to Scotland in a caravan. Pete Don and Evelyn and myself. We stayed the first week in Ayr the second week in the Tummel Valley. Don took us sightseeing most days. One day I was in the shower Don turned the tap on nearly scalded me. I fell our of the shower and caught myself on the cupboard I was black and blue all my right side. I sensed a man at the side of me laughing.

We went out the next day to Lake Gilped it was exactly the same as the vision I had with Evelyn. It was really surreal.

I stopped smoking on the 21st November and I was sitting watching television when I had Pete's father appear beside me and tell me to get Peter to the doctors, Pete said he was fine but two days later he had a heavy bleed, Peter was diagnosed with bowel cancer a week later and was operated on the 12th December all he had as treatment was Spiritual healing and Paracetamol.

I never ever disregard anything which spirit gives me. He recovered well and went back to work but had gone back too soon he developed a hernia which was quite painful. The doctor said he needed a repair sooner rather than later, so an operation was scheduled for two weeks later in Louth.

He went in and whilst recovering again something happened which was so bizarre. Maria and I went to visit him when in the car travelling, we felt a spirit gentleman's presence in the car. He said he was going to the hospital so could we drop him off. Maria talked to him all the way there, which was very strange, and then he was gone.

Peter spent his recovery counseling two men who had been diagnosed with bowel cancer who were not coping very well. Again, spirit with a helping hand. He helped them to look at cancer in a better light.

This was a time of changes again; I had my heart attack I thought I had heart burn but no definite heart attack. I was taken to the hospital this was Father's Day 21st June 1999 at 6.45 pm. I was at church giving the reading when it felt like an elastic band snapped then pain.

I carried on with the service and afterward Maurice and Sally gave me healing. I arrived home Pete said I looked ill so I went to bed. At 10pm he checked on me did not like the look of me so rang 999.

I was blue lighted to hospital and was out of it for three days on a machine, all my family came in and out, so I was never alone.

Spirit was very quiet, but I know I was getting healing. I received beautiful flowers from my brother Keith although we were estranged.

I had lots of healing by Maurice and Sally they came to the hospital, also Lynne Merrills she came too to give healing as she trained with me,

One of the funniest things to happen was, my daughters brought my grandchildren to visit, I was sitting by the window and as I looked down I saw Lynne coming to visit. Lynne always wore a long coat and boots. I said to my grandchildren David, Jamie and Kristina, Come and see Mary Poppins the look on their faces when she came into the ward was a delight.

In the hospital ward as I recovered, I gave healing to a lady in the next bed her name was Christine. She had been diagnosed with cancer, I talked to her also another lady about spirit which I feel I was put there at the right time and right place.

After I left hospital, I visited Christine at home and gave her healing and talked to her about life after death, which she wanted to know. A year later she passed but was ready.

I managed to get back to work in September which was good, and I had started to lose weight which was great. But have, to take a tablet for the rest of my life. Thank goodness I have not had a relapse.

Mastercare closed in January 2002 so had to transfer to another site Techguys still part of the Dixon group, this was great I enjoyed the extra responsibilities. I stayed there till I retired in 2009.

This was also a time of moving forward. Travelling and meeting new people, when we went to Canada June 2003 it was great met with Rita and Peter Browning and travelled around Canada meeting different people. It was a time of meeting minds.

Rita and I went to Lilydale in Buffalo a spiritual sanctuary it was brilliant just seeing where spiritualism began, also I met a couple of mediums from uk who rented a cottage for the season giving readings I have met one of them since.

The next two years we went back to Canada, spent Labor Day at Lake Nepawassi near Barrie, and went to a wedding on the lake there, and went to a concert to see Cher wow was a wonderful time.

The following year we went back, and Rita and I and two friends went to Lilydale again. This time I worked on the message stump, healed in the healing service. And gave messages on the platform.

This time we stayed in a haunted house. The doors kept opening and closing and lights and orbs all round the room, It was amazing tiring but amazing.

The funniest thing was when you closed the door the door opened, I closed it and it opened again and it closing, Rita says leave it then the door opened. I ducked when an orb flew at me. Yet I laughed because why duck, yes why?

I saw again spirit here a little girl waving to me in the meditation, as clear as day. I beckoned her over and opened my eyes she stood in front of me, a little girl ages about seven wearing a white dress covered in flowers smiling she then faded away.

I went into the hall for the service I was announced as the British visiting medium where I was given the second part of the service. I remember giving a reading to a large lady in the middle a colored lady. I saw a river with lots of houses being pummeled by water, she acknowledged that houses had been engulfed by floods a few years ago.

Also, I said it was more recent and I heard a lone singing voice singing Amazing Grace. She said her Grand'Mere was Grace and she sang in church. I gave her other evidence which was great. So brilliant.

The next morning, we went to the six o'clock meditation, healing and went for breakfast before leaving the lady who I read the day before said there was a hurricane in New Orleans last night where she lived by the river, it had flooded her house. Premonition?

The next amazing thing we did was to be invited to a celebration on the Six Nations Indian Reservation. The dances and the colours where out of this world. We saw Teepees and Indian dresses and bonnets which we will never forget. The service was a closed to welcome the new chief, we were told not to photograph the ceremony, Peter did the camera never ever worked again.

We then went to a large barbecue where Pete was given his first Buffalo burger, It was as big as his hand he had trouble eating it. I had fruit as I was vegetarian. We shook hands with the chief and was invited back anytime as friends of Peters were friends of his.

Rita and I then went to the reservation to learn Metamorphic touch healing and sitting in a drumming circle wow, wow, wow the energy was beautiful.

I must say the best parts of Canada was seeing Niagara Falls, seeing Cher, meeting people who are now great friends. Also doing church services in Bancroft, giving messages in Hamilton, and Scarborough. This was the last time we went to Canada as Rita and Peter went their separate ways.

I did two divine services in Bancroft. The first one was a fellowship service where the congregation brought a plate for lunch. Some delicious food I had never tasted before. These services were given differently to the English, but my evidence was taken.

Pete at this time was given a boat and taken to the lake to go fishing for Pike and Bass. Peter sometimes went as well. They often brought the catch back when we would have a meal of the cooked fish.

We went to Hamilton for an open platform Rita, and I went up to give messages. I spoke to one lady who only spoke French, but I managed to convey the message which was great. Afterwards the booking secretary wanted to book me for the next year. Unfortunately, we did not go back.

One night in Hagersville I did a flower service in Rita's home for her circle they had not seen a medium work so was again a learning curve for myself and for Rita. She started her own spiritual path and is now a reverend in Canada and has her own church which again was part of spirits own ideas for us.

I also did a few private readings which gave me some spending money for when we went to Port Dover for a day out. This was a place on Lake Erie where sand was brought to make a seaside resort. Every Good Friday all the bikers congregated from all over Canada. They spent millions of dollars on food and biking equipment.

Another Bizarre thing happened Rita and I spent some time in her basement she had turned into a reading and healing room. She had her computer also a lounger, and music center. We had a meditation half hour every day. Music playing. Rita had not been working long, halfway through she went into a trance and started talking in a different voice. She gave so much information, when the meditation finished, she could not remember a thing.

I feel it was my way forward learning and experiencing new things and meeting new people. Spirit shows you new, things every day.

Living my Life the best I can

7

Pain is a warning also a lesson

I think I am honored to work with the spirit world as they are with me leading me and showing me many wonderful things, also giving me words, which help me and also help others on their journey of spiritual life. The first channeled words where so profound not only words for me but for Paul he read every word I wrote. There was always something to share that would help other people. Later in this book I will share some of the words I received.

I was very tired and was not only working overtime everyday at my job. I was running a private circle on Tuesday nights, healing and sitting in circle on Wednesday night, and sitting in Lynne's circle on Thursday nights I was not sleeping well and was beginning to look haggard. Sally kept on saying to me I had to slow down, or the Spirit World would slow me down.

On 21st June 1999 I was doing a reading in church when I felt an elastic band snap within my chest, I gasped and carried on. I was not aware this was a heart attack; I had slight pain but nothing major. Maurice gave me some healing and I went home,

Peter knew I was not well and kept his eye on me, he phoned the doctor at 10 pm but they sent an ambulance I was to stay in hospital for ten days to recuperate. The doctor was very good and when I was back on my feet, I went to Nottingham hospital for an Angiogram which was horrible but my arteries where clear.

My God this was a shock not only to me but the system I had put on weight maybe because I was happy, but this weight was not good for me, so I cut out sugar and other bad things out of my diet and started to lose some weight. I was feeling better and went for healing every Wednesday, so I was getting back into Sync, but as I was later to find out the changes were coming.

The spirit world was in charge my life was in their hands. Hazel Abey a Spiritualist Medium asked me to go to Spalding to practice on the platform Easter Sunday 2000. I gave three messages which were accepted I was so delighted. We then went to Boston Church she did the philosophy then told me she was ill and left me to it, so amazing I was now a fledgling Medium.

I then started to get bookings myself and by 2003 my diary was getting full, not from me asking but from word of mouth I was getting phone calls from spiritualist booking secretaries as congregations were telling them about me which was really nice, and to this day I do not promote myself.

I then started to accept bookings to do psychic suppers which were interesting, and I began to work with Pat Brown doing charity Medium Rally's which again promoted us and we raised in three years around £12.000 pounds which was great.

We decided to go to Cyprus to expand my knowledge but because I was afraid of flying it was a challenge all was booked then my brother-in-law died of a stroke so we could not go.

And as I had met a lovely lady in Canada on the internet Rita Browning, she was researching all things spiritual so as we began talking, she invited us to Canada and as my roots were in Canada, I was determined I wanted to go so did a flight to Cyprus and went to Canada end of August beginning of September 2003 to stay with Rita and Peter a new chapter.

Canada was so beautiful Niagara Falls breathtaking I saw so much and met so many lovely people. In return I taught Rita all I knew which helped her on her spiritual journey. I gave all of me she took and gained knowledge.

The following year, we went in June and took a trip up to North Ontario and spent a couple of weeks at Lake Nepewassi, relaxing on this beautiful lake shore in a log cabin. Pete and Peter with Al went fishing every day,

Jean Rita and I had circles and I taught them all I had learnt. This was a time of learning for me too. I now know I am a teacher and that my life was planned and that the direction I take is directed by Spirit.

We also went to a workshop about training your mind to mediumship, this lady was around 7o years old with tremendous knowledge. She helped me no end and often when I am teaching her words come to mind. Reaching up to spirit will reap rewards.

The following two years we travelled to Canada I went to Lilydale Spiritual centre in America, and I gave a demonstration at the message stump and served Hamilton, Scarborough, and Bancroft Churches. This was so amazing as I sat in a physical circle and stayed the night in a haunted house and felt the spirit, I really want to feel that again.

The circles where then my next thing to do I took over from Pat and Jane and held the awareness circles for the next five years, some particularly good mediums came through the circles and are working around the churches and doing well. I had to give them up as my spiritual journey has changed, I am booked solidly two years in advance.

Our holiday to Cyprus was an eye opener as I had never been abroad before. We stayed In the Roman Hotel. Peter had Salmonella poisoning and ended up in hospital, it did not stop Evelyn and I exploring. We would wave to Pete as we went out. He got a better tan and he had his bed on the balcony;

I went underground in the Valley of Kings I had to leave I could not bear the death and feelings I was getting. Later I asked spirit why I felt that way, I was told the people who entered the shrine left their emotions behind. I was picking up this because of my spirituality.

We next went to a place up in the mountains stopped for a mezzie as I was a vegetarian they substituted meat for Halloumi cheese and potatoes cooked with cinnamon, I gave the lady next to me a reading with psychometry she was amazed as all I told her was correct.

We went on holiday to Malta we were sitting in the bar when someone who had seen me working in a charity Rally on the week previous told them I was a medium, talking to me and asking questions, where did it all come from? I gave the woman a reading in a back room when I brought her family through, she realized wherever we are a medium can connect.

I had people asking for readings I could not say no, and I found the language barrier no problem, they were lining up I never charged, When I was able to connect, I thanked my guides for the helping hand they gave me.

We then went to Tunisia; we went to one of the trips out I met someone from church Then the following year we were in the Canaries in Fuerteventura the same thing happened. So now when I go on holiday, I ask to be given a bit of space.

Life is now good I enjoy working for Spirit and Spirit enjoys working with me, so a new chapter has begun in my life. One thing I am sorry about my sister Jackie, I did not see her before she passed in 2010, Also I have not spoken to my brother Keith or my sister Sandra, families, we where close in youth but estranged in years. I will now give you some of my words from spirit and encounters.

I spent a lot of time with my sister-in-law Evelyn we were two jokers together, both Librans and both of us have a lot in common. Her daughter Sandra always called us the naughty schoolgirls which I suppose we were. We liked the same things, so when we went on holiday she came too after Don died.

One time when we were in Fuerteventura on a camel ride we laughed at the least little thing. We walked for miles feeding the chipmunks and met like minded people. Pete seemed out on a limb as we did things which was a time of relaxing. I did give readings to the friends we made and loved it as it was practice for me. One lady still comes for a reading.

Pete and I decided to go to Tenerife for Christmas one year it was an absolute wonderful two weeks. We walked we slept and really relaxed. It was 100 degrees on Christmas day. One day we went to a banana plantation I got bitten by a beetle my face blew up so the rest of the holiday I had black eyes but I would go back there in a heartbeat I needed this holiday.

Spiritual Gathering

8

Words from the Spirit touch the soul and open the heart!

Perfection of the spirit
2004

To strive to be perfect is every spiritual person's ambition but to us in the spirit world we do not expect this, we want you to be the best you can be always but considering the behavioral patterns of the like-minded people on this earth plane, there is often things that do not go in the order of things.

We often wonder where we went wrong. Did we push you too hard did we stop over achievers going forward? We are at a loss to know this, as we have many channels on this earth side that push their selves forward and teach others of their ilk, but often they change our wording, so they do not listen to what is within.

Life has many discouragements and many joys, but which is it? What do you see, what is it like to see discouragement in our children's faces or the slope of the shoulders of our spiritual people? Do you see what joy is? Rejoice in our name we will show you the way.

Many teachers walk this pathway, many teachers show the way, students listen and act, but what are they listening to? is it our word or is it your word. Let each of you let go write our words how they should be. Knowledge is forthcoming listen. Hearts are meant to be broken but also to be mended.

We will be your teachers if you will listen, the song of the spirit will be always with you but all the knowledge you will learn, some the hard way but most the spiritual way.

Hearts, and voice together as one. Unity, of spirit and man, we will become one.

Love and hope for the next generation of elder's earth wise and spirit wise each to work together on the tree of knowledge, voices to proclaim our word, so listen to the inner voice. We will give you our undivided attention as we each earn the respect of each other.

God Bless everyone the spirit has spoken

The words where coming fast and furious and I was writing it all down, spirit said you are the editor listen and write our words.

I then started doing workshops especially with colour. aura graphs, encaustic art and flower readings. I asked for direction for my workshops they gave me all I needed. These words where given to share.

What is Colour?

- Colour pays a big part in our life. Why?
- What is Colour Therapy?
- How does Colour relate to physical problems?
- Methods of using Colour.
- How does Colour deal with the body?

Red
Red is natures warning Colour. Red can indicate a high level of emotion, such as impulsiveness, aggression or hate. It can also indicate pain, swelling or injury on the physical body. Red can also on occasion indicate a very

strong willpower or energy being directed to achieve personal goals. When looking at the aura this can often be seen as red ball shapes in the upper part of the aura. This is also the base Colour when used in meditation.

Orange
Orange is an outgoing Colour warm, spontaneous, courage and joy, also shows in someone who likes to be social, outgoing and like to be around people. If a muddy shade of orange is seen on the body, nearing a brown Colour, this can mean a severe condition, muddy shades elsewhere around the aura can indicate emotional imbalances, pride, vanity, and worry, and around the head mean laziness. Pastel shades can indicate searching for new spiritual paths, and aspirations.

Yellow
Yellow is a mental Colour in the aura. You will see this Colour around the head mostly more than any other Colour. It signifies concentration, thinking, learning, and studying. It also can indicate spiritual learning, usually on the pale to white shades. Muddy yellow can signify fussy over bearing natures and behavior. It can reflect being overly critical about others, or attention seeking.

Green
Green is nature's growth, the Colour of renewal and healing. Healer's doctors and nurses have green in their auras. Those with green in their auras usually have calming balancing effects on others and are generally well balanced themselves. Strong, straightforward, and protective. The heart is the focus on this Colour. When green shades of blue are seen in the aura this indicates emotion physical or mental abilities. Muddy green indicates jealousy, possessiveness and untrustworthy.

Blue

The lighter brighter shades of blue are at the throat chakra. This generally reflects good imagination, creativity, and good intuition. It is a calming peaceful Colour; it can indicate the ability for Clairaudience. The deeper the shades of blue can indicate loneliness. The muddier shades can indicate blocked perceptions, worry, sensitivity, fearfulness. Royal blue indicates honesty, truth and good judgment

Indigo, Violet, Purple

These three colours are associated with the third eye the brow chakra and the crown chakra. Basically, this is spiritual knowledge put into action. These colours will be present in people who meditate a lot, channel and work on the spiritual path. You will always find these Colours around the head, changing to lavender and into pure white this indicates a higher spiritual learning. Muddy shades can reflect erotic imagination, overbearingness and needs of sympathy.

Pink

Pink is associated with compassion, love, companionship, and emotions. This Colour is belonging to the heart chakra also mixed with green is true spiritual love and strong companionship.

White

When white stands out in the aura strong and well defined this is indicating pure energy, life force, truth and purity. Mainly found in yogis and gurus, and indicates strong awareness of the individual with cleansing and purifying. You may see speckled white around healers and mediums healing or demonstrating this is also showing that spirit energy is about.

Black

Black is usually a warning Colour it does not mean death or dying, but of illness or injury. Usually emotional imbalances such as depression. It can also show in the aura as damage or a hole needing repairing. Sometimes you may see black when reading an aura on the appendix when they may have just had them out, so do not think there is anything bad in seeing black.

Gold

Gold in the aura means spiritual strength, and spiritual energy. This is a wonderful Colour to protect from negative energies.

Silver

Silver in the aura is like white in the aura the Colour of the highest spiritual energies or spiritual forces. The highest realm of spirit or of the angelic kingdoms is the pure silver with sometimes a mix of white and gold. To see flecks and flashes of silver in the aura is as seeing flashes of white pure energy. Pregnant women have silver sparkles in their aura, not all women with silver sparkles but pregnant ones.

These channeled worlds helped so much with allowing me to work in Lincoln, Worksop, Hull, West Bridgeford and Grimsby churches to introduce newcomers to Spiritualism.

The people who participated were so enthusiastic so understood where the Spirit and colour where connected. They understood to meanings and were able to communicate with others.

Again, this is where we take what we need and leave the rest behind. I went back to basics with Pat and Jane and that was the best thing I ever could do. I found more about myself, and lots of comings and goings but my life was getting better, and my spiritual side being developed, and knowledge was being imprinted into my brain which my brain was a sponge, the more I got the more I wanted.

I also heard my sister had died, I was devastated but because the family was estranged, I had not seen her for 5 years, and she only lived an hour from me. This made me feel why was this so hurtful, as they decided to remove me from their life, Keith Sandra too. But families are like this.

I started to work the platform and working in the circles, again it was taking its toll I was tired. I stated drawing faces and giving readings. A lovely medium Mary Hall served Lincoln Church I was given words for the divine service as I was chairing. She said please may I have your reading as it is so true.

This was the reading

Choices

Many are the choices we have to make in this lifetime, we ask many questions of our parents and of our teachers, and often we do not get the answers but have to wait a lifetime before the right answer comes.

Yet how many times do we know the answer before the question is asked. This is the beginning of enlightenment. The opening of the mind to new possibilities, the two worlds joining together to bring in knowledge.

How many of your children when they were growing, asked a question and you did not know the answer, but had to search to not only pacify the child, but to find the answer for yourself, but now after opening your mind and asking, the same question the answer is forthcoming because you asked. You did have the choice then to seek the right answers, but now you know you only have to ask and it is given.

This is the meaning of life itself.

How many of you have to make a choice, on what you need to do with your life at this present time, a job change a change of home, you make the choice but have you made the right choice?

Then when you look back over your life do you see the decisions you have made, and do not know why you have made your choices, then remember you had freewill to do as you chose not as others chose for you.

So now as you walk your pathway, remember you were pointed in that direction, so nothing happens by chance. Everything comes down to choose, what is yours.

This medium was a lady that gave short messages all were spiritual messages, she never ever gave me a message, her words were" spirit will give you your message ask."

I met this lady again when I was working in Grantham, I gave a message to her which was well received, she said "I knew you were going to be exceptional" so good praise indeed.

The next I started to get readings by word of mouth at first, I gave them free as it was a learning curve for me. Each was received very well. Then the other mediums on the circuit said I must charge as I was giving my own time.

One medium that helped me as well as Pat and Hazel was Jenny Johnson, she used to make me laugh so much. We only met up when we were at suppers, but she rang me, or I rang her. She always had something to say. She sent her son to me for guidance. I was devastated when she passed, although she has been back and given proof.

Another lovely spiritual friend Is Pauline Richardson another exceptional medium who always gives of herself. Whenever we went to a supper, she brought her husband of 51 years to sit with Pete they got on like a house on fire always putting the world to rights. Another was Dawn Brace her husband always took time to sit with Pete were the three of them would sit talking all through the night.

Open your heart and listen to your soul

9

Life is a working of the mind

Then the words started coming some lovely philosophies I write what I am given, sometimes a word other times it is an item.

BEING TOGETHER IN HARMONY

Long ago the pagan religion was the main religion on the earth plain, where druidism was one of the highest cults they worshiped the land, mother earth was the focal part of their worship, and the land was good. The trees and the rocks held the energy from the sun and the air was clean. Then the religion split into many, and the world became disorientated, but the earth stayed good.

The Indian nations worshiped the Great Spirit, and they took to look after Mother Nature, with chants and meditation, the land was then again good, and the generated energy brought out the hidden depth of the earth. You must now sit and remember what it was like to worship the sun, moon, and the stars. And when the air was clean, and the land was good. Then the earth was that of plenty the rain came to quench the thirst of the earth, the plants grew to feed the multitudes of this world and the earth was good.

Now in your religions you must remember to ask for help in your prayers, for self-enlightenment as it was in the beginning, so your planet is again good. Then the energy within yourself will be a blessing from the earth a harmony from within and it must be allowed to develop fully, to enrich all the lonely souls who are in need.

The healers must be allowed to develop their gifts more deeply and to call on the guides and healers to work more closely with them to heal the entire disharmony within.

As it was in the beginning so it shall be again with help from the world of spirit as more people become enlightened, so more guides and helpers strive to bring knowledge to this world to nurture the land for all.

The guides tell you to use your senses, to listen to the world and what it is trying to tell you about the land and all who reside upon it, and when you can do this and can send out your thought to help then you have passed the test. A blessing for each one of you, you all deserve it.

So, my friends if you understand what we are trying to tell you then you are enlightened, and now you have a greater knowledge from within, and the earth will again be good.

I read this at Louth Spiritualist Church for the Remembrance Divine Service, I started to read when the medals fell. Which was either a coincidence or they were not attached properly.

I then started to have some dreams some very strange also I started to hear voices clear in different voices and accents, I still do, but not hearing more so no further.

Here are some of my dreams as I wrote them down.

24/12/04
I saw a wall of water come over a wall. I was in a shopping Centre trying to find some curtains. I was by the sea. I looked across to the window, the sea was higher than

51

the window all I could see was water it covered to whole place everybody was screaming we couldn't get out, just people crying. Two days later the Tsunami in Thailand. Premonition?

18/09/10

I dreamed I lived in Three Holes or Prick willow I had a toddler she had blonde curly hair. Every time I have dreamed this dream the baby has been a baby this time, she was nearly four years old. Always I have wondered about changing nappies I never seemed to have any. I worked in a factory and my little girl was in a crèche she was not far away from me. It was nearly home time, and I was waiting for my mother to pick us up.

I went to get the child her coat and she had messed herself I cleaned her up but could find no nappies. I left her on a little potty and told her to read her book and if she wanted a wee to use her potty. I then asked someone in the next room to keep an eye on her whilst I went for Pampers. I reached the shop which was an open all hours shop and asked for pampers for a four-year-old, it was like asking for the moon. Young children were serving in the shop one adult in charge. The man sent a thirteen-year-old up a rickety ladder onto a shelf to bring down a plastic container with trainer pants.

I went to pay for them nobody to take my money when I went back to the room the container was missing; no one seemed to know where it had gone. The shop owner came and asked where my package had gone but to no avail. She reached up to a rack and came up with a beige brown pair of tiny tot frilly pants which she charged me one pound. I thought I saw another pair but no it was a frilly purse which the shop owner took.

I went outside to find my mother she was not there nor was my little girl; I had been searching for these pants for a whole hour. I woke with a sea of faces who I did not know and feeling disturbed and had a heavy head. I have dreamed the same dream three further times.

20/12/10

I dreamed I was walking down a street it was in the countryside. I was alone but I could hear rumbling. The moon was shining I do not know where I am going but I was hurrying. Suddenly water came rushing down the road, the riverbank had broken, and water was rushing down the road. I looked at the sign it was Market Deeping. I don't know whether there was a flood or one to come. But I felt the water was covering me, so it was definitely a flood. Maybe past when this area was a flood plane.

13/12/15

I dreamed I was in Tunisia on holiday. I went into the hotel there was a conveyor belt that took you to your rooms. We had to sit on it with our cases. When we reached our room, Pete was ill I had to go and get a doctor for him. I sat on the conveyor it took me into a large room. People where milling around and standing over by the bar was the man, I had lived with Ernie Booker, I found myself ducking so he couldn't see me. I awoke in a sweat.

Life continues forward not back.

10

Time to take charge of your life

How do you feel?

How do you feel today? Did you wake up not feeling refreshed you have tossed and turned all night, your dreams are troubled, and your head feels as though a thousand drums are hammering in your brain. Did you have to have that last glass of wine? Or eat the curry at midnight?

Did your mouth feel chalky and dirty? Did you have to smoke too much with your pals?

We abuse our bodies daily with what we eat and drink. And later on in life we regret what we have done, when we suffer a stroke or we have a heart attack. So what can we do?

1. Firstly, treat your body as a new-born child nurture and teach it.
2. Do not smoke it ages your skin and kills the good antibodies in your blood stream, and causes bad breathing, good lungs keep you in top working order.
3. Moderate your drinking; too much, damages your liver and causes other problems such as again heart attacks and strokes.
4. Cover up your body in high sun, skin Cancer kills.
5. Watch your weight grease covering your arteries can give strokes and heart disease.
6. Exercise when you can as this can keep your heart healthy.

I found I was well over my natural weight; I had stopped smoking in 1997 and was immensely proud of myself I had smoked since I was fourteen so to stop by myself was a great achievement. I had begun sitting in circles and was looking to learning and working with the Spirit world.

My Husband Peter had Bowel Cancer December 1997 two weeks after I stopped smoking, but I completely believed in my guides who said they would work with me to stop me smoking for good. Even with the stress I did not start again. Peter was successfully treated and was given wonderful healing which is continuing to this day.

At the same time Pete's Daughter in law Megan Angelo's wife was diagnosed the same. The cancer spread to her brain which in turn sent her into a coma she passed May 13th, 1997, she was 36 years old, she left a son and a daughter she had no life. She was beautiful inside and out.

So, when I started to gain weight, I just put it down to stopping smoking, I had a heart attack out of the blue 21st June 1999. As I said in earlier chapters. I was taken to the local hospital and was diagnosed with Angina which I would have to have medication for the rest of my life. The damage was to my mitral valve.

So, what we need to do is train our children from an early age to take care of the borrowed body. Eat healthily, watch their weight, do not self-abuse. Life can be good if we listen to our self.

Maybe as we as mediums sense when someone needs a helping hand, we say thank you to the great spirit for showing us the way. The healing is part and parcel of our development, So, my healing started when I realized I had to do something about my weight.

I feel we are here to make a difference and we do. We are here when a person wants a helping hand. So many people came into my life foe help and healing.

In September 2012 Pete and I spent a week with Suzanne Graham and family at Soham. We had a few days out which was nice. One night I was in bed sleeping in one of the single beds, Kai was in the other, when he started screaming and ran to his mum. I opened my eyes standing by my bed was my late husband, Alan. He pointed to the door. He then disappeared. I wasn't frightened I was amazed as it was the first time of seeing him. He was dressed in a grey jumper and looked well the last photo I took of him he wore the same.

In November Suzanne and Graham split up due to his infidelity so again premonition?

I was having really bad pain in my hip so was sent to see a rheumatologist Mr Joshi he diagnosed Fibromyalgia. He sent me to The Lincoln Hospital to have an injection under anesthesia into my hip this was a terrible thing I had pain in all my bones.

I now must take Gabapentin and Co-Codamol as I was allergic to Tramadol. Thank goodness that was addictive. I did find an ointment made from hemp that helps when the pain is bad in my hip.

Fibromyalgia is a very debilitating disease headache, not sleeping, pain in different parts of the body, nausea, and crippling fatigue. Sometimes so bad I had to go back to bed just after getting up and slept for two days. One day they will find a cure for it I am sure.

It has taken a toll on my health as the migraines started again the auras and pain. The doctor said it was to do with the fibro but gave me some tablets to take when the aura comes. The headache came or I had pains in my stomach then sick for an hour so dreadful knocks me for six. One lady in boxed me and said you are healer heal yourself. It doesn't work that way, but I do ask.

I find an infinity to crystals too so have a few healing crystals. I also bought a beautiful crystal book which I am finding the different crystals used for, different ailments. I have made up some crystal healing cards which I share on social media. A couple of my favorites

No 5
Amethyst...Spiritual Awareness
A purple variety of the quartz family all sizes and colours of light and dark. Used in meditation it promotes spiritual awareness and guidance. The larger amethyst stones placed in a bedroom helps to cleanse other crystals by placing on top. The amethyst also helps to open the crown chakra and the third eye in spiritual circles. Today use amethyst to help find your own awareness, on a spiritual level. Feel the power emitted from this stone to bring clarity and insight to find who you are. Also use amethyst to re-program clear quartz.

No 14
Clear Quartz....
This stone is classed as the master, especially for healing, It is also used in other work. Casting spells, to transmit energies by energising the body to amplify and receive like a radio receiver. Spirit also sends their thoughts through the quartz crystal to those who are receptive. Using the crystals around the body during healing helps not only to heal but also to promote healing, to energise all the chakras. So today either use the quartz to help to balance and harmonise your own chakras to bring healing and health to you. Or to help you to transmit healing to those who need.

Soul Groups

11

Colour and teaching helps the soul.

21 Jan 2011 Words given by spirit.

The law of averages says every day we meet someone of our soul group; we feel infinity with them at once and know that we have seen and sought that energetic bond between us. I meet many people on my travels around the churches I serve in this lovely country of England. I always seem to know when I meet a person whether the person met is a good egg or a bad egg. This is found in the perception part of the aura.

Challenges are often given to us to know who and why we are given these souls but in an ideal world we would be given the perfect person to grow with, alas this is not always the case. We are hurt and disillusioned, but this is a learning curve for us ourselves.

I run a teaching circle and each person that comes to me I find are quite different, they each are seeking knowledge and want to know why this; and why is that happening to me. I do not profess to know all the answers, but I can always trust in my guides to help me to give what is needed. Sometimes I am at a loss, but I rest assured that at the end of the day that answer will come.

When we sit and meditate, I ask each to look into their minds eye and see what they can see or use the imagination to bring those wonderful colours to the front of their meditation, the pupil loves the way these colours make them feel. I love to work with the colour energy because all that there is there, is true colour.

The colour and sound working together gives great meaning, to the spirit world and I find when music resonates through the soul it reacts to the soul colours. Look at it in this sense Doh Rah Me Far Soh La Tee Doh Chakra red orange yellow green blue indigo violet and white. Together with healing in the body and the soul they work together.

When you look at a garden full of spring flowers look at the colour yellow, you will be so amazed to see how many butterflies go to the colour yellow, this colour resonates an energy which is the chakra solar plexus the healing energy on the human body, also on the aura. It is a special colour which is warm full of energy and is the Centre which guides the soul to perfection, as this colour travels this colour is usually seen with the naked eye, followed by blue and then red.

These are the primary colours.

I like to work with colours especially with wax and as they are spread on card tell a story the same way as a clairvoyant works with the spirit world. The guide comes forward in the same way and teaches with colour. And as you look below you will see how the colours tell the story.

As you look at the picture notice the colours the rainbow also how the colours swirl together. To me it shows the spirit open to reflection and how strong colours represent the soul's journey. This, in a manner of speaking is learning on a higher level.

This is another where you can see faces and other noticeable things

As we meet up with our soul partners sometimes, we know in an instant we have met before, we have that special link. Why that is; sometimes is very confusing, as is déjà vu seeing a place and knowing you have been there before. I know I went to Waterbeach in Cambridgeshire in 1964 I knew that I had been there before. I took my husband to a place where I knew there was a forge; there had been many years before, so why does that happen?

Another place was Looe in Devon I recognized that place I had never been there before, that was in 1989 before I started to have the interest in Spiritualism. So again, Soul Groups Soul Partners all coming from different areas of the country, or reincarnation what do we believe in.

As we learn we grow and not only in our own personal learning but on our Soul Groups learning. The soul learns and when meeting kindred soul, we pass on the information not by speech but my mental sharing. This is how I understand the teaching.

Sitting with Spirit asking the question what Soul Groups are. I did many workshops teaching colour and connecting with the spirit world to direct and find yourself. I found also working with pastels and crayons to work for Auragraphs. My students seemed to like to get dirty but were able to connect. They each connected with others so knew they were connected to their own soul groups.

Two of the best places to teach these was Hull and Grimsby, I started to set up in Grimsby there should have been 10 people, Pete covered the floor with his dust sheets we were all getting ready when another 5 arrived. It was good workshop, but I was tired as I had the service at the night as well. Jim Cork had a go and loved it.

Hull always had a few and as I had the service after they always gave a good, yummy lunch. The students there were a breath of fresh air they enjoyed the camaraderie, the laughter was contagious. I still have a few of them as friends on my social media.

One was in Cambridge arranged by Ann Fordham they loved the concept, and all enjoyed working with the Encaustic waxes. One lovely lady called Mary was able to connect too and was able to give messages. She passed to spirit not long afterwards.

I also gave my circle members a taste of working with colour. One week we would do encaustic art and read for one another. The following week we would do Auragraphs by tuning into one another drawing and reading for each other.

People came and went from my circle as they learned they moved on. Some for mediumship but others just to join other circles. I had one couple who used to love to come but owing to illness had to stop coming but always had the healing.

We learned to connect and draw psychic art where one lady could not draw but wrote a piece for the person she was sitting with all was always spot on, she did not get pictures but words.

One of the best one we had was sitting in the red light and seeing if we could connect with spirit past life, Interesting but I did not go down far enough. I did find out that I had passed with a plane coming down on top of me so I passed in the war and was born in the war.

Timing and finding what is next

12

Never disregard the soul's choices.

My thoughts
Bridges when they are broken are made to be re- built
Lives that are damaged are made to be healed.
Families that are challenged are meant to be helped
Children that are broken are made to be fixed.

At the Christmas season comes to heal the world
We look back on our sorrows and try to mend the rifts
Families so broken cannot find the way
To say I am sorry, and it will not happen again.

Life is full of broken promises and healing needed by all
At this Christmas season meant to be full of joy
But alas full of sorrow, hurt and upset
When will it all end, to see a joyful sunshine?

Healing of souls to broken to hear the cry
God the great redeemer sits by your side
Healing broken families as he holds on to you
Time to mend the bridges broken yet can be fixed

A few broken promises cam be made to hold fast but true.
Trust in your inner spirit, and love your mortal realm
Let tomorrow bring the healing of broken hearts and more
Families brought together to bring love forgotten by all

In our time of sorrow ask for the healing for mankind.
You are all worth the promise of good to follow the bad,
Rejoice as you here your spirit within
Say you have done well follow your dreams.

Change...

It is a time of change dears and a place of woe
As we walk in the shadow of destruction,
Mother earth has started to show
She will take no more nonsense.

Her wrath will bear no shame
Millions hurt and injured
Time to take stock on our world now
See what mistakes have been made.

Help Mother earth to re-consider
It is up to us as to share
The gift of healing for our earth
And live-in safety for evermore.

So blessings from the spirit
As we help to bring in our healing
Bringing the changes for us all to bear.
The brunt of our own battles

Minds hurt and being misdirected
We ask the healing angels
To bring healing for mankind.
And for all those with mental issues.

We help all we can but,
We cannot always see
Who are suffering in silence?
But who are being set free?

So today send out all your love
for all those suffering minds.
Bring peace for those in solitude
And ask god for the health for mankind
Time to rest and find me

The Oak

The Oak stands so proud and true
In a field all alone
Rabbits, dancing back and forth
Mother Nature singing in one tone.

The daisies flowering year by year
Never planted by one hand
Re-growth is part of nature's plan
In this free loving land.

Part of nature's regrowth plan
Comes naturally to all
Green fingers and summer rain
As Mother Nature's new re-call.

As children make up daisy chains
Wrapping round each hand
Underneath the major oak
Each make their stand.

Nature in this fair green land
Trees in all their splendor
Our children growing to progress
Each with the gifts to flower.

The oak bows down his hefty branches
To all who need shelter from the rain,
Peace and tranquility
Is Natures song and refrain.

Remembering and bringing in the words

13

Poetry the soul's blanket and ease

As We Return Home...

The days we live in this world of ours
We wonder where time has gone,
Days, years months not hours
Another few then we will be done.

We should make our mind up what to do
To follow our chosen path or not
Keep our thoughts so pure and true
To see if we have learned our lot.

We make our plans in our head at least
See the marks we have certainly made
Sometimes we see that untamed beast
Have we? do we think made the grade.

We now as spiritual earthly souls
Have learnt our lessons or we hope
We have reached our chosen goals
So as we return, we can show we did just cope,

We have done what we set out to do
See the brightness of our learned souls
The inner spirit has learned lessons too
And has reached those hidden spirit goals.

Sometimes we leave early
Not had time to live
Perhaps our soul was weary
But had much love to give.

The family we leave behind
Grieve with so much sorrow
But the love left is defined
We did not beg steal or borrow,

So as our soul leaves this plane
To travel on to somewhere new
All the memories it did gain
Will stay to learn anew,

So goodbye dear soul we say
We have left our mark
Shouldering our sorrow today
As we each sit in the dark.

We reach up to the light ahead
Arms outstretched to reach
Our loved ones gone in ahead
So they will begin to teach.

The way our Lord wants us to be
To sit at his right hand
Our soul is now surely free
To sit in his company so grand.

Remembering

Tis', the time of remembering
All that have passed and gone,
November is in passing
The time of life that's done;

Mothers fathers brothers
Lost and gone to God.
He surely takes good care of them
Mother Father God.

He sees them and love is given
As their lives are all done
remembering all our families
Who are dead and gone.

Life is just a passing
of souls that are left to find
Their stories of love and honour
With a love so blind.

As all of us together
Fighting in our wars so blind
Finding not only glory
But a love so hard to find.

To swell with remembering
All that have passed and gone.
Fighting for love and freedom
Now brother, father son.

The poppy is that symbol
for fighting for love and truth
As our soldiers fought for glory
And pass out living proof.

Remember all that are lost to us
not war but illness too
The past glories are dead and gone
Whom are left just a few.

Remember the passing of our angels
Children gone too soon
Giving of the symbol
The poppy the life gone to soon.

The Recognition of Spirit
Lest we forget.....11/11/2013

90 years in the service of our country man and boy girl and women, we have spent many lifetimes under and overachieving but what have we in answer to this time we have had despair we have had anarchy we have become a proud nation and can hold our heads up with pride. Children of Spirit we can hold our heads up and say we have achieved our recognition, or can we?

Wars in 1918 wars in 1939 wars deliberate and added to, wars in the Middle east the Falkland's in Iraq, now in Afghanistan so much loss of life why did or why do we need these wars? Why do we need to show our superiority are we in tune with ourselves and our spirit within no I think not we are set alone the human, race? We are magnanimous as a people we want to be able to stay proud and just show we can stand proud, in the wake of adversity, but often we do not need this. We have enemies in this world, and we make enemies, we talk treason, and we accept treason as it is. We stand for our country and yet we stand apart.

Spirit and the elders of the spirit world ask of each of you to still be a proud people, be at one with each other but look back at the suffering and the early departure of many souls to the higher side of life when it was not needed. You are all better people in this world now enlightenment has reached all, a tremendous beginning the time of learning is at hand a pathway opening up to each and every one of you. So, listen to the self.

Spirit recognition and the recognition of the self is the beginning yes stand up for the true meaning of loyalty, love... hope... peace and harmony this is your beginning your walk into a peaceful world, tread carefully send out those thoughts bring in the peace for all time. Recognize Spirit and that you are the true Spirit within…..

The Challenge.

There once was a fish called Haddock
And his mate called Plaice,
decided to have a challenge
in a ten mile race.

Haddock had a wager firstly
ten bob on the nose,
Plaice did one better
as the saying goes.

Prawn was on the starting block
his pistol raised and ready.
Crowds all where cheering
the noise was quite heady.

They then set off on their journey
neck and neck together,
round and round the corner
before they took a breather.

The spectators where cheering loudly
Haddock was out of puff,
Plaice striving for supremacy
And getting in a huff.

Forwards backwards forwards
each one taking the lead,
when suddenly they faltered
Someone else was in the lead.

The friends saw it was a flounder
Racing faster and faster
They fell back in anger
This was a disaster.

As to win the money wagered
both Haddock and Plaice agreed
To go back to the beginning
The flounder must be in need.

To race again in challenge
never never again they agreed
to stay within true friendship
Never to take up the lead.

The moral of this story is
To take time out and rest
No one fish is better
but each one is the best.

The Moon

The moon creates a balance
shining way up high
showing all the beauty
as she glows in the sky.

To all that walk upon the earth
bringing peace to all
listening to sister owl
as she makes her call.

Open to all the heavens
like music to our ears
the moon shines her shadows
helps to overcome our fears.

She shines with bright shining gladness
Upon all on earth she sees
At night when its cloudless
She certainly does not cease.

She travels on till morning
when with the dawn comes the sun,
sinking slowly downwards
Until the day is done.

Then eventide she rises
to shine silently on mother earth
Moonbeams shining softly
on new life giving birth.

The angels gladly greet her
women, children also cry
as they see the goddess moon
As she travels across the sky.

On the shadow of the morning
and on the birth of l life
God created this heavenly beauty
the universe with love for life.

Sometimes when I receive words I maybe anywhere in bed
in the middle of the night, I always have a notebook by my
bed. In the loo, in the car. I stop and listen to the words,
sometimes I haven't paper but spirit always bring them
back.

One time I was in the car park of the doctors waiting for
hubby to come out all I had in my mind was scrub, scrub ,
I asked why again the same words. So I sat with my
notebook and this came.

Housewife's Chores

Spick and Span scrub and scrub
Clean the house rub a dub dub.
Daily chores I am not a fan
But I have to do it when I can.

Dinner cooked ready to eat
Into the kitchen to find a seat.
Rice and curry chips and stew
Not a lot left so now I'm blue/

Washing machine full to the brim
Ready for the wash oh so grim,
Next the dishes to be washed
Hands sore skin all squashed.

Making the beds oh what a chore
Back bent and so sore,
Bathroom next this I hate
Scum on sinks I don't rate.

I think now I will have a rest
It looks spick and span I am the best.
Facebook open time to scroll
I am now so on a roll.

Something serious sometime funny.

When I was at work the lads would ask me to write
something about them which I did. One was for a man
who was leaving so I wrote a poem about him and framed
it. It was Captain Pugwash. Which was about him and his
life.

So many lost souls

14

The light is out time to move forward.

It has been an incredible journey the last 25 years where I have developed and given so much help to people in need. Churches opening and closing, my own where I developed gone, nobody to start new development.

Bracebridge Heath opened a church in Lincoln so we can breathe a sigh of relief for the new generation. It was the brainwave of Nolan Barnes and Ben Davies out in Potterhandsworth. He promoted a lot of mediums and the people started moving away from the main church as some people did not like the church services, so paid the money for the alternate mediumship messages only.

Ben left to train as a doctor, so Nolan moved the church to Bracebridge Heath where it continues to prosper. I do a few of the services during the year especially if I am not busy when there is a cancellation. I am on the doorstep.

I started to move a bit further away further north to Deneby, Sheffield and Mexborough. Then South to Wisbech, Peterborough, Cambridge and Dereham. When we went to Dereham after the service Pete fell over the doorstep and broke his nose, he drove all the way back to Lincoln with a carrier bag. And a toilet roll nose bleeding, to Lincoln County hospital where he had his nose plugged. Hence, we have not been back.

The next few years where a blur I was working full time, serving churches Saturday and Sunday nights, and more often in the week as well. Also running a circle in my home on a Thursday night training other upcoming mediums to serve on the platform, Some Tuesdays I managed to make it to Carols circle where I could sit and enjoy the peace as we took it in turns to chair.

I had a taste of sitting in trance with a red light but would not let go, although I was over shadowed. I was able to go so far but I trusted in my guides sometimes I am in an altered state when I write.

I did a service one night with flowers at Spalding Ivo Centre run by Cathy and Michael. This night there were quite a congregation all had brought flowers and laid them on a table. One bright spark had brought a cannabis plant. Spirit picked it up straight away and the message was about addiction. So, they always pick up on things as I did not know it was cannabis.

I had another service one night for a Woman's Institute, out in the Lincolnshire Wolds, they had a speaker once a month on a Wednesday evening. I did my first one with flowers. None of them had seen a medium work and loved it.

A few weeks later I was booked again to do a clairvoyant evening with psychometry. There were eighty people there and all brought a variety of items which were laid out on the table.

I was drawn to a painting of a house in a field, real vibrant colours. I was shown an old-fashioned double bed that was broken. The lady who brought in the picture laughed and said "I had my wedding night in the cottage. When we got into bed it collapsed, and they had to spend their honeymoon on the mattress on the floor."

This was great confirmation as the whole place erupted in laughter. The lady was 90 years old, and her husband had passed the previous year and he was giving me the information. I went back there a few more times until it closed its doors.

Another clairvoyant evening was in Harris Street Peterborough I was working with a psychic artist called Lynne. We were working well together. Lynne was drawing another picture when I picked up a gentleman called Eric, he was giving so much information. He was the President of the church and had passed that morning. So, an enlightened soul. My first time there but not the last.

Another Clairvoyant evening was at Love Lane Spalding a flower Service. All had brought a flower except one man he brought a bag of plain flour. I gave him excellent communication from his father which shows if spirit works with you, whatever you are given you are always able to connect if you trust.

I often worked with Pat Brown we did charity evenings in different places, Also Medium rallies to raise money for Parkinson's disease, Cancer and for the hospital. Different mediums often worked with us.

Another way to raise money for charities was psychic suppers where again we worked with different mediums, Louth, Wisbech, Spalding where the best ones also Pams at Worksop. And Worksop's SNU church for pie and peas. This was also a way for mediums to catch up with one another.

Over the years I am pleased to say spirit has worked well with me and the conversations I have had have been many. I often sit with a pencil and book and write down all I am given. From messages and for poetry and philosophies.

Taking time to sort my life out has taken its toll. Living loving and losing. By losing my stepsons have taken a lot from me. Alan when he passed was a shock as he had been with me from eight years old. He went through a divorce missing his girls, he had issues with his mind, but had started getting his life back and then taken before his time.

Then Angelo he fell asleep after having an operation he had overcome Polio and other issues and again gone before his time. A man that loved his two children he had lost his wife to bowel cancer in 1997. But believes in the afterlife.

The pandemic started 2019 Covid 19 it was named. My stepson Colin had stomach cancer he passed 2020 in November. He believed in healing but alas the healing did not work.

It made me wonder how stretched spirit must be with all the passing to the higher side of life. Over a million lost just from the United Kingdom. At least the wonderful scientists found a jab that kept it away. We suffered a lockdown when humans went stupid, clearing the shops of essentials, so much thrown away.

I have been hearing direct voice so many times during lockdown and being kept indoors. Voices that I heard clearly, then in my mind's eye people standing by me. Changes coming again I was given a word then a philosophy and poems were coming.

Breaking my arm was a real time of challenge and change. Pete had to do more cooking and cutting up my food. This made me think of all the really disabled people having to rely on others. Lots of making myself do things I would normally not do.

I was asked to do a Zoom service online I worried about it but trusting in the spirit it went well. I saw people again that I had not seen for a year. I offered to do readings online again the connection with spirit helped me to bring their family and friends for them. I also went to the different online churches, one of the best was Yataheeh in Leicester. It was like coming home. Since then, I have done services, quizzes and met other mediums.

I then decided to join the online group for spirit art, a lovely meditation wit Veronica Jenkins and then in rooms to connect with another person, it was brilliant drawings that were accepted, also drawings I could accept.

So again, changes that are coming. The philosophies are stronger the drawings better, I know my guides are with me and I trust. I am also booked up to the end of the year with Zoom and in person.

One thing though I find I am more empathic, to hear a song or to hear a sad story I find I am in tears. This is spirituality and spirit drawing close. I feel when they need me to connect with someone, so my Peaceful waters helps with this.

The Pandemic

A couple of pals went out for a walk
To relax walk and to talk
About everyday bits and bobs
And wonder about the loss of jobs.

Alas said one making it clear
There will be no more jobs I fear
Shops are shut all stock left
Bars and cafes left bereft.

Covid 19 has taken all spaces
No jobs left for all races.
The loss of life never to be filled
Money for those left will never be billed.

The government always trying their best
To compensate for those at rest.
Some of them shout in one voice
The human race has no choice,

But to fight and fight and stand tall
As death I am afraid is always on call.
The names of the weary
The virus eating at the teary,

Time to ask for a spiritual aid
For families suffering the death the virus has made.
To help us to understand
That the peril that befell this land

Can be overcome with time
If the vaccine is given in time.
So banish the virus help us heal
I implore the humans in a strong appeal.

Bring back the life we had before
The pandemic gone but left us raw.
So goodbye to 2020 and 2021 madness
Help us to heal and leave us with gladness

Be more aware of the human race
And come together but still make space.
By Christine Stewart 17/2 /2021

Palm Sunday

He rode upon a donkey
Riding triumphant as a king,
This day bringing love
As the crowd all did sing.

Jesus is our saviour
His disciples walked beside
Him on his little donkey
As he did his lonely ride.

He was told what would happen
As the uncrowned king,
Yet he was so saddened
As the crowds did sing.

As he rode into Jerusalem
Palms strewn along his way,
Head held high as he rode
Triumphant so they say.

Palm Sunday as its called
That a man would be king
Palms strewn across his path
Triumphant songs they did sing.

He was called the king of the Jews
As Pontius Pilate made a plea,
For all prisoners to be brought forth
But Jesus did not flee.

So, this holy week was over
Triumphant he did come,
As the crowds chose Barabbas
Wrong choice said some.

So, Jesus was a mortal
A beautiful perfect soul,
Jesus to be our saviour
A perfect now immortal Soul.

As Easter now we remember
As Jesus now does come
Into our minds more often
Our Saviour now says some.
Christine Stewart 28.3.21

A Spring Garden

As I sit in the garden
Watching all the birds
Scratching in the flower beds
Looking for the worms.
As the spring rains bring them to the top
The birds picking them all up
In their shiny orange beaks
For their baby birds to feed.

I look at all the flowers
Coming into bloom
Daffodils and tulips
Colourful all hues.

The washing on the lines
Blowing in the wind
Then an April shower
Have to bring them in.

I love the spring garden
As the new life comes in force
A bee making a beeline
For these colourful blooms.

As night draws in
The birds go to roost
In my new nesting boxes
To bring up their brood

A lot of these poems and readings and philosophies will be put into my next book which will be poems ditties and spirit words given. I know I saved a lot of words from spirit so now I will be able to share them.

Stephen Rowland inspired me to publish my book as after reading his spirit words I knew I could pass them on. His book is worth a read.

Also, Tom Kings account of his spiritualist journey we always get inspiration from others, as we meet so many on our path,

Life continues at its own pace

16

Trust is a word to live by.

In 2014 Peter had a heart attack, it was not a bad one which was lucky. Peter was in hospital for two weeks to recuperate as he was diabetic. I cancelled my bookings as I had no means to get there.

I thought I would have to pack up my church bookings as I do not drive. Peter was not allowed to drive for the time being. He recovered well thank goodness but was diagnosed with angina.

Two friends who where in my circle developing at church when I was running it, asked if I took them on the platform, they would take me to my services. Rita Rymer and Elaine Jennings, they are now working mediums and I am so proud of how far they have come.

I started a Facebook page in 2015 with a friend Ruth Stallwood, where likeminded people could share poetry, paintings, and philosophy. Also, they could have a free reading.

When it first began, I had a few readers who would give time out to give the readings. The same people would ask for a reading every other day. I had to make some decisions as they were living their lives on readings.

I changed the readings to once a month yet still the same people without fail, are asking for readings as soon as the month is up. We now have 653 members, although I have removed some over the time, for not leaving feedback.

It is now 2021 a change has come upon this world a pandemic has overcome us millions upon millions dying all over the world. Covid 19 a terrible time for us all. Spiritualist were asking spirit why?

My stepfather passed in February 2020 breathing difficulties which we think was covid. My daughter June let me know as nobody told me. I did not go to his funeral as the first lockdown was in force, so I was self-isolating as I have a heart problem.

I was walking in my garden moving a hanging basket to put by my back door, when I fell, I don't know whether I stumbled was dizzy or was just clumsy. I cut my nose and fell on my left elbow. I had to get myself up and go to find Pete as he couldn't hear me.

I went to the hospital at 9pm had x-rays they said all was ok. I was sent home after having blood tests and an ECG test, it was 5.30 am Pete wasn't allowed with me because of the covid.

My arm was numb, and pain in the wrist and hand but the doctor said just to take paracetamol. My arm was black from the shoulder to the wrist.

A week later a specialist from the hospital rang me and asked me to go to his department as they had found a break. An appointment was made at 10 am. On arrival I was sent to the x-ray department and then to have my arm put into plaster.

The specialist said it had been missed as it was my funny bone. Another appointment was made for a month. It was a dreadful time I couldn't move my arm; I was sleeping with my arm in the air. Pete had to help me dress and cut up my food. Again, my guardian angel.

At my next appointment I was sent to have the plaster cut off, an x-ray and to see the specialist. He made me an appointment for three days later to be admitted into hospital to have bone fragments removed and manipulation under anesthesia. Then appointments for physio, to help heal.

I did a good job of breaking my arm and getting my arm to move again. Also, to see an osteopath Jonathon Hobbs on the Birchwood. He helped me to be able to straighten my arm to how good it is now. And is ongoing helping me with my hip.

This was a change spiritually too as all churches were closed, not allowed to sing. Also, space between people. Not allowed to visit family or friends it was a nightmare. So, from March 2020 all was stop. People dying from Covid was affecting many people, so as churches were closed there was no comfort.

When Colin died only immediate family were allowed to attend as I was step mum, I had to watch the service on Zoom it was not the same as I could not be with Pete as he broke down. Losing one child is bad but a second was devastating. The service was still lovely.

Churches did not give up though Zoom services were born. I as a platform medium had to change my way of working and most of 2020, I was busy most of the year either services or joining open circles. I made many new friends too.

Christmas came and went I managed to give some presents but in the new year lock down was eased. But alas not to last long as the virus was taking more lives as a new variant came

I was working more and more on Zoom in Ireland, Scotland, America as well as churches who I was booked for live services I did online. One service I did at Yataheeh Church was Encaustic art, I was able to work with the pictures and send them through the post to the recipients.

The lockdown ended and we were able to get out and about only to be shut down again. I had a hair appointment to be cancelled again for another month.

2021 services all online as the lockdown was still in force but gradually it was relieved churches could open for 30 people but wearing masks was essential. If it keeps you safe wearing the mask I will wear.

My first service in the flesh was 16th May at Bingham only the minimum amount but it was such a lovely feeling to be in a church again. Also, a couple more in May maybe it was going to get back as normal.

Both my June and Suzanne visited as they were able, but it is terrible not to be able to see my grandchildren. The younger ones won't remember me, so that hurts. Maybe soon we will get chance to visit ourselves. The worst of this not being able to give them their Christmas presents until well after Christmas. Bur that's a pandemic for you.

I spent a lot of time doing readings online which again was working very well. I was able to connect and received lovely feedback. Some of which I will share with you.

May 17/2021 Jayne Wheatley
Thank you so much for the amazing reading, you gave me so much evidence that only myself and Ady only knew. The depth of what you told me blew me away to prove that life goes on after passing. It was so heartfelt, and the words used only Ady would say to me. You left me feeling very much loved and extremely blessed. 100% accurate,

and you told me things only me and Ady knew, so bless you big love and Squeezes xxx

28/6/2021 Sandra Craven Nottingham
lovely reading from Christine, a medium who is approachable and candid, and most of all well attuned with spirit. The digital online reading worked a treat, and it felt as though we were in the same room. I was able to view and choose my cards, and christine also sent me an audio recording of the full hour long reading. Lots of accurate names and evidence of loved ones here and in spirit was given. Christine was able to give independent advice and insight into a difficult situation I was Experiencing, Many Thanks 🙏

Sandra Chapman 11/7/21 Lincoln
I recently booked to have a reading done by Chris, because of the lockdown this was done by Zoom, It was amazing. I have known Chris many years through spiritualism, I've watched her work and she never fails to surprise me with her wonderful spiritual gift, She truly is an amazing person. At the time of booking this reading with Chris, I was very stressed with some things and desperately needed some help and guidance, Wow Chris helped me, she was just amazing I really was an emotional mess this one particular day, her knowledge and help from spirit that worked through her was phenomenal she helped me so much. I have had readings from Chris before and she never fails to help. She is my go-to medium. Thankyou Chris from the bottom of my heart. Sandra xx

Carmarthen Spiritualist Church 8/8/21
A huge Thank you to Christine Stewart from Lincoln for filling in a cancellation this week. It was lovely to meet you for the first time too.

A great evening was had by all with lots of evidence, memories, and advice. You were on a roll. Hope to see you again soon

Kellie Capel 28/8 2021 London
Thank you for my reading it was spot on and could understand everything. I could also take all the names and evidence given; I came away very happy with my reading Thanks again. XX

Keith Hubbard 28/8 Online Circle

I did a reading for Keith on Zoom listening in was his circle members. Each took something from his reading. Keith accepted all but the next hour talking about more random things the circle got an insight into a medium working with a medium. All evidence was taken., he was pleased with his reading and all the evidence given.

28/8/2021
An evening of clairvoyance on Spiritual Psychics TV this was a challenge, yet it went very well I was in a room by myself with a producer talking to me and helping me to connect. I worked for an hour and a half giving evidence and receiving confirmation. Afterwards I was so tired but happy. Over 1.7 thousand comments. People on SPIV Facebook and U Tube so look forward to my next.

Printed in Great Britain
by Amazon